Original title:
Arbor Awakenings

Copyright © 2025 Creative Arts Management OÜ
All rights reserved.

Author: Helena Marchant
ISBN HARDBACK: 978-1-80566-721-6
ISBN PAPERBACK: 978-1-80566-850-3

Nature's Gentle Awakening

The flowers yawn as sunbeams creep,
A squirrel dances, oh so deep.
Blades of grass tickle the toes,
While ants in suits are striking poses.

Birds croon tunes, a clumsy song,
A peacock struts, he can't go wrong.
With every bud, a giggle blooms,
Nature chuckles, clearing gloom.

Cherished Moments in the Canopy

The trees don hats of leafy cheer,
The bees march in with buzzing beer.
A woodpecker's drumming makes me laugh,
As chipmunks launch their acorn gaffe.

Sunlight dapples, a playful smile,
While snails are racing, in slow style.
Nature's playground, what a scene,
Where laughter's echoed, bright and green.

Breaths of a Rejuvenated Wood

The breeze whispers jokes to the wise old pine,
A tortoise squeaks, "I'm feeling divine!"
Clouds roll in for a slapstick routine,
While the frogs croak punchlines, it's quite the scene.

The owl blinks slowly, a sleepy fella,
"Whoo are you?" asks a giggly acella.
Roots stretch and wiggle under the sun,
As every branch knows how to have fun.

The Return of the Green Guardians

The hedgehogs don their spiky crowns,
As rabbits joust in leafy gowns.
The guardians chuckle at playful feet,
"Come join the dance, don't miss a beat!"

A wild hedgerow whispers silly tales,
While squirrels trade their tugging sails.
Fungi break into a disco move,
In the forest's groove, they find their groove.

Canopy Dreams

In the woods, the squirrels chatter,
Filling the air with silly patter.
Trees sway in a playful dance,
While birds join in with a cheeky glance.

The branches stretch like arms so wide,
Whispering secrets with leaves to confide.
Laughter echoes as roots tap feet,
Nature's joy is a funny treat.

Tender Leaves of Tomorrow

Tiny buds peek from bark so shy,
Wondering what it's like to fly.
With a wink, a breeze gives a shove,
Pushing them into the world with love.

Some leaves giggle, some leaves trip,
On the dance floor, they all take a dip.
Mistakes are made, but oh, what fun!
Under the sun, they sparkle and run.

The Secret Life of Trees

What do trees do when we can't see?
They tell tall tales of being so free.
Some wear goggles, some sip on tea,
Plotting their pranks, oh what a spree!

At night, they giggle, they twist and shout,
Rooted in mischief, they can't live without.
Whispers of bark and echoes of glee,
In the world of green, it's a wild jubilee.

Nature's Gentle Resurgence

After the winter, they poke and prod,
Plants stretch and yawn, giving a nod.
Grass tickles toes, flowers burst into grin,
Spring's slapstick show is about to begin.

With a hop and a skip, the blooms prance around,
Their colors more vibrant, they spread joy profound.
A daisy trips over its own little feet,
In the garden's laughter, life feels complete.

Nature's Rebirth

The squirrels plan their grand parade,
With acorns stuck in their capes.
They giggle as they serenade,
Each branch a stage for their japes.

The flowers blush in hues so bright,
As bees buzz tune in a tangle.
The trees sway left, and sway right,
Dancing with a joyful jangle.

The sun plays peek-a-boo all day,
Tickling leaves that burst with glee.
As nature rolls out her ballet,
Everyone joins—come, see, come see!

When rain falls, they all take a dive,
Splashing mud in a careless spree.
With every sprout, they feel alive,
In nature's playful jubilee!

Sunbeams Through the Branches

Sunbeams tickle the leaves' green tips,
While shadows play hide-and-seek.
The branches wiggle in their grips,
Sprouting giggles, so to speak.

A butterfly in polka dots,
Flutters by with a cheeky grin.
It teams with ladybugs in spots,
Creating chaos, a funny din.

The owls are snoozing, snoring loud,
Dreaming of acorn delights.
While squirrels gather a raucous crowd,
In wild chases under starlit nights.

As sun sets low, stars start to glow,
The trees whisper silly tales.
Of mischievous winds that blow,
Echoing through the night trails.

Life from the Dormant Soil

Beneath the earth, a party's planned,
Worms groove to their own sweet tune.
They dig around, a wiggly band,
And laugh at the mouse in a balloon.

Seeds crack jokes as they sprout wide,
With roots that tickle and twist.
They spring up tall with playful pride,
Claiming their space, none can resist.

The beetles boast of strength and might,
While ants share news about a feast.
In secret chats till morning light,
They're nature's jesters, never ceased.

When rain arrives, they cheer and sing,
Announcing spring's delightful plot.
With every sprout, they joyously swing,
As life bursts forth from its hidden spot!

The Shimmer of New Life

A dew drop winks upon the grass,
  Her charm is hard to deny.
The daisies gossip as they pass,
  'Is that new posture a sly try?'

Little buds bloom, they strut with pride,
  With petals flaunting colors wild.
The bees are busy, lost in the ride,
  Turning blooms into floral smiles.

The frogs croak out their best refrains,
  As crickets join in with a beat.
Swirling around in garden lanes,
They dance their way to summer's heat.

And when the sun sets on the fun,
The night brings out the stars' delight.
  They giggle softly, one by one,
  For in the dark, the world's just right!

Rebirth of the Silent Boughs

A tree once slept, now wakes with glee,
Its branches stretch, just wait and see.
Squirrels prance, with acorns to toast,
They dance on limbs, like hosts at a roast.

A trunk that creaked, now cracks a grin,
As birds make nests, and chatter begins.
Laughter spills through the emerald air,
Where leaves tickle whispers, beyond all care.

Echoes of Leafy Dreams

Leaves giggle softly in the gentle breeze,
They plot with flowers, in playful tease.
A breeze swoops in, like an old prankster,
Making all petals dance, oh so gangster!

Dreams of photosynthesis kick in at dawn,
While dewdrops sprinkle, like fairy spawn.
They sip from the sunshine, a morning toast,
To the leaf and the bud, let's party the most!

Secrets of the Swaying Branch

Watch as the branches shake and sway,
Whispering secrets, they laugh all day.
A rustle here, a giggle there,
An acorn's joke dances in midair.

Frolicking fawns sneak under the shade,
Telling tree tales that never fade.
The trunk just leans, amused by the fun,
In a world of bark, we're never done!

A Symphony in Green

In a concert grove, the leaves perform,
Their rustling tune, oh how it's warm!
The roots beat drums, thumping below,
While the sun beams down a radiant glow.

Sway to the rhythm of nature's song,
Join in the revel, you can't go wrong.
The branches conduct with flair and twist,
A melody of laughter, you simply can't miss.

Blossoms in the Breeze

Petals fly like tiny kites,
They swirl and twirl in playful heights.
A bumblebee with silly tricks,
Dances round like it's on flicks.

The trees wear crowns of leafy green,
Their branches wiggle, what a scene!
Squirrels leap, they look so spry,
As acorns bounce like popcorn high.

The sun chuckles, beams so bright,
As flowers yawn with sweet delight.
A playful breeze runs through the park,
Chasing shadows till it's dark.

Nature's giggles fill the air,
Each creature skips without a care.
With laughter loud, they all agree,
It's a riotous jubilee!

Verdant Revelations

A sprout peeks out with a wink,
Saying hello, don't you think?
Giggling grass beneath our toes,
Penning jokes with every rose.

The thorns are jesters, full of cheer,
With prickly jokes, they draw us near.
A raindrop lands, a plop and splash,
Who knew puddles could make such a splash?

The flowers hold a silly talk,
As butterflies do their own walk.
They tell of dreams in sunny skies,
While clouds just chuckle, rolling by.

Leaves chatter on their lofty stage,
In the wind, they turn the page.
Laughter echoes through the leaves,
As nature tricks and never grieves!

The Awakening Canopy

Branches stretch with sleepy yawns,
Whispers wake up early dawns.
The sun peeks through with a grin,
Telling trees, let fun begin!

Nests of birds chirp goofy tunes,
Crooning laughter 'neath the moons.
Insects boogie on their feet,
Underneath the leafy sheet.

The squirrels play a game of hide,
As shadows flit from side to side.
With acorn hats and nutty pride,
They scamper fast, no need to bide.

Giggles spill among the roots,
As part of nature's grand pursuits.
A canopy of stories spun,
Where every jay is out for fun!

The Dance of Renewal

Nature's stage is set to sway,
With twirling leaves in bright ballet.
The wind's a jester, full of flair,
A swirling twirl without a care.

Caterpillars strap on shoes,
To party hard with morning hues.
They wiggle, giggle, flip about,
While bees buzz loud, a happy shout.

The blossoms tease with fragrant bursts,
As nature quenches all its thirsts.
With playful quirks, they bloom and jest,
In this wild dance, they feel the zest.

Each twig and branch plays hide and seek,
As laughter plays atop the peak.
With every twist and joyful sound,
In this grand dance, joy is found!

The Arrival of the Green

Tiny buds peek out, they wink at the sun,
Dancing in breezes, oh, isn't this fun?
Leaves whisper secrets, they tickle my nose,
A leafy parade as the green army grows.

Squirrels are plotting, with acorns in hand,
Challenging pigeons to a race through the land.
The trees shimmy gently, they're laughing, you see,
What a hilariously verdant spree!

Stories of the Seedlings

Once upon a time, in a dirt-filled pot,
A seedling cried out, "I'm ready, why not?"
With dreams of tall trunks and leaves that collide,
A squirrel just chuckled, "You wish! Take a ride!"

Tiny sprouts giggle, sharing their tales,
Of sunbaths and raindrops and mischievous snails.
"I grew an inch!" one exclaimed with pure glee,
While worms rolled their eyes; oh, the hubris of thee!

The Unfolding Canopy

Beneath the tall branches where giggles reside,
Laughter's like shadows, where secrets can hide.
The sun peeks through gaps in a leafy embrace,
A whimsical dance of green scarves in space.

Clouds drift above, with a soft puffy grin,
While birds tell their jokes, let the fun times begin!
Branches stretch open, like arms wide in cheer,
Inviting all creatures, come play, gather near.

Echoes of New Beginnings

In the heart of the grove, where the fresh shoots are bold,
Come gather, dear friends, for the stories unfold.
The crickets are crooning, their nightlife attire,
While toads hold a concert by the moonlight's fire.

As morning dew sparkles like diamonds on leaves,
The whole world awakens, as laughter retrieves.
In this comical forest, where mirth reigns supreme,
Every tree shares a giggle, living the dream.

Garden of Gentle Resurgence

In the garden where veggies conspire,
Tomatoes are plotting, oh what a fire!
Carrots are giggling beneath all that dirt,
While peas in their pods joke in green skirts.

Sunflowers are dancing, their heads held up high,
While radishes whisper, "Oh me, oh my!"
The lettuce is blushing, it's feeling so bold,
In this place of fun, nature's stories unfold.

Bees buzz with laughter, just buzzing around,
With flowers in hats, oh what a sight found!
A garden of whimsy, where all things do play,
Where veggies and flowers just brighten the day.

The Awakening Earthsong

The soil awakens, it tickles the roots,
Worms wear their party hats, oh what hoots!
The daisies are humming a brand new tune,
While daisies and dandelions dance 'neath the moon.

A chorus of frogs joins in on the fun,
While ants have a picnic, oh aren't they the one?
Crickets click-clack as they keep up the beat,
Nature's orchestra comes alive in the heat.

The grasshoppers leap with a jig and a jive,
Creating a ruckus, feeling so alive!
The world's in a whirl, so alive and so bright,
In the symphony of spring, all takes flight!

Cradle of New Life

In the cradle where seedlings stretch and unwind,
A broccoli's dreaming of being well-timed.
With peas that have plans for a baby food feast,
And zucchini laughing, claiming, "I'm the least!"

Chickens are clucking, oh what a great day,
With feathers a-fluffing in the sun's golden ray.
The corn stalks are gossiping, tall and so proud,
While roots drink the jokes that the soil has allowed.

The daisies are chuckling at ants with their loads,
And frogs in the ponds are practicing codes.
This cradle of life is a fanciful place,
Where laughter is woven in nature's embrace.

Trees in Bloom

Amidst the tree tops where laughter is found,
Branches are giggling, oh what a sound!
Buds are bursting forth with a bashful grin,
While critters are scampering, inviting in.

The poplar's winking at the clumsy old oak,
The willow is whispering a ticklish joke.
Cherry blossoms twirl like confetti in air,
While squirrels tail spin, unaware of the dare!

With sunlight a-sprinkling on leaves up so high,
Fruit trees are eager, their bounty nigh.
In this playful forest, so merry and bright,
Nature's humor tickles from morning till night.

Renewal Under the Sunlit Canopy

Under the trees, squirrels play,
Chasing shadows all the day.
They leap and dart with silly flair,
Wiggling tails, without a care.

Sunlight filters through the leaves,
Tickling noses, making thieves.
Nuts and acorns in a race,
A couple's breakfast turns to chase.

The birds are singing tunes so bright,
Hiding worms with all their might.
Worms wiggle, dance, and twist so fine,
Waiting for their lunch divine.

With laughter echoing through the glade,
Each critter joins the vibrant parade.
In this fun-filled leafy bliss,
Nature smiles, it's hard to miss!

The Dance of Sprouting Buds

Tiny sprouts in little rows,
Pop their heads where sunlight goes.
With a wiggle, they say, "Look!"
Nature's own little storybook.

Dancing twigs with playful sway,
In the breeze, they twist and play.
"Oh me, oh my, a flower's out!
My outfit's fabulous, no doubt!"

Worms below do cheer and shout,
"Join us in this sprouting route!"
"Let's show the world our mighty green,
We're the starlets of this scene!"

Each bud unfurls with joy and fun,
Twirling 'neath the warming sun.
In this garden, laughter's heard,
The universe is one big bird!

When Shadowed Slumber Ends

Awake, awake, the shadows flee,
The sun peeks through, a jolly spree.
While sleepy things shake off their dreams,
The morning burst with giggling beams.

Bunnies hop, all spry and cute,
Chasing each other branch to root.
"Is it spring or just a prank?"
They tumble down into the bank.

The lazy cat, with yawns galore,
Stretches wide and snags a snore.
But listless dreams now slip away,
As sunshine greets the bright new day!

Listen close, and you will find,
The garden's laughter, sweet and kind.
In this cheerful waking sigh,
Nature chuckles, oh so spry!

The Promise of Blooming Life

Here comes the bloom, in colors bright,
Giggles sprout in morning light.
Petals chat and start to tease,
"Wait till you see our grand degrees!"

Bees come buzzing, quite the show,
"Hey, flower friends! Let's spread the glow!"
They tickle blooms with feet so sweet,
Turning work into dance and beat.

Each blossom beams with story told,
Of sunny days, both fierce and bold.
"I've got pollen, you've got flair,
Let's throw a party, everyone's invited here!"

Gaudy greens and fragrant hues,
Wave and sway, spreading news.
Life's a giggle, color and cheer,
All's well among us, every year!

The Breath of Spring's Embrace

The trees are giggling with glee,
As buds pop out, a sight to see.
Squirrels in tutus twirl and leap,
In their leafy stage, they love to peep.

Daffodils dance in the warming sun,
Caterpillars munching just for fun.
A puppy in diapers chases a bee,
Oh, Springtime! You've set the critters free!

Raindrops fall like musical notes,
Slippery squirrels in tiny coats.
Frogs in hats jump with delight,
Throwing parties all through the night.

So let's join in this uproarious cheer,
As nature laughs, loud and clear.
In this wacky world where joy's not rare,
Come dance, come sing, without a care!

Rebirth Amongst the Boughs

The branches chuckle, wearing new greens,
Flowering pajamas, nature's routines.
Bunnies donned in shades of bright pink,
Chasing after clouds, oh, what to think?

The bees hold meetings on petals so wide,
Discussing their plans over honey pie.
While acorns gossip about winter's end,
Whispering secrets that they can't pretend.

A crow in a hat caws puns from above,
Jokes with the deer, spreading laughter and love.
Joy fills the air like bubbles in stew,
Every rustle and chirp brings something new!

So let's raise our voices, let's make it loud,
Join the merriment, join the crowd.
Nature's playground is ready to play,
With laughter of spring, hip-hip-hooray!

Blossoms of Hope

In gardens aglow with colors so bright,
Butterflies flitting, a whimsical sight.
Chickens in sunglasses strut about,
Even the flowers are dancing about!

Tulips so sassy, with hip-hop flair,
Daisies are giggling in the warm air.
A snail in a shell that looks like a car,
Zooms past the daisies, a superstar!

A parade of ants donning tiny hats,
Sing songs of the spring while battling mats.
Piglets in bowties munching on treats,
Making the rounds on their little feets.

So let's celebrate with a quirky shout,
Nature's comedy is what it's about.
Join in the laughter, spread it like glue,
These blossoms of hope, let them bloom true!

Echoes of the Forest's Revival

The trees throw confetti, their leaves twirling round,
Echoes of laughter resonate through the ground.
Witty raccoons in masks come to play,
As the forest wakes up from its slumbrous stay.

The owls share jokes from high up in the pines,
While sprinkling wisdom in quirky lines.
Chirping the news of a bright sunny day,
Tickled by sunshine, nothing dismay.

The pond's having parties with frogs in a line,
Wading and splashing, oh, what a design!
A turtle offers rides with a wink and a grin,
While fish toss confetti, inviting us in.

Echoes of joy through the vibrant trees,
Nature's own symphony carried by breeze.
So come join the fun, let the laughter roll,
In this silly, bright world that brightens the soul!

Beneath the Bark of Time

What tales do trees still tell,
Of squirrels and birds who yell?
They whisper secrets, quite absurd,
Like ticklish leaves and a singing bird.

In summer sun, they tell their jokes,
About the rabbits, the mischievous folks.
Each gnarled root has a life of its own,
While ants make plans for the great unknown.

The knots and grooves, a laugh or two,
A woodpecker's rhythm, a funny view.
With branches stretched in a silly spree,
A tree could really host a comedy.

So next you walk beneath their dome,
Give a chuckle, feel at home.
For every sapling, tall and stout,
Has a punchline waiting, no doubt.

Swaying with the Spring Winds

As breezes dance with leaves so bright,
Trees twirl around in sheer delight.
They giggle soft, they wobble proud,
A leafy conga, underneath the cloud.

The branches sway with silly grace,
It's nature's dance, a funny face.
A pine tree tips its hat with flair,
While willow wiggles without a care.

The blossoms laugh, they bloom and cheer,
With colors bold, oh dear, oh dear!
The bees join in, buzzing a tune,
All swaying together, like a cartoon.

So grab a twig, let's twist and spin,
Join the merriment, let the fun begin.
With every gust, we sway and clap,
Nature's stage is set, with a funny rap.

Petals in the Morning Light

In the dawn, petals start to bloom,
With colors bright, they fill the room.
They stretch and yawn, oh what a sight,
Like sleepy heads in morning light.

A daisy winks at a passing bee,
'Buzz off, my friend, can't you see?
I'm busy here, no time to chat,
Just holding tight to my comfy hat.'

Tulips giggle as they sway,
They love to play peek-a-boo all day.
Fluttering soft in the gentle breeze,
Cracking jokes with the playful leaves.

So raise a cup to the flowery crowd,
Who laugh and joke, so strong and loud.
With every bloom, there's fun to find,
A morning show for the cheerful mind.

Nature's Awakening Serenade

The morning chirps a silly song,
As nature wakes, we all belong.
With croaking frogs and chattering birds,
The symphony plays with quirky words.

The flowers hum a cheerful tune,
Competing with the whistling tune.
A bunny hops, a foot-stomping beat,
Nature's band, oh what a feat!

Trees join in with rustling leaves,
As the sun climbs up, everyone believes.
Fat little bugs with a jazzy flair,
Tap dance along without a care.

So as you roam this lively scene,
Join the laughter, feel the keen.
For nature's serenade is here to stay,
An orchestra of fun, come swing and play!

Nature's Gentle Resurrection

When winter's chill begins to flee,
The squirrels dance with glee.
They scamper here, they scamper there,
In search of nuts and fresh warm air.

The birds return with songs so bright,
Hopping around, they take to flight.
The trees once bare now sport their hats,
As nature laughs and chats with bats.

But don't forget the muddy shoes,
As blooms burst forth to share their hues.
A garden party soon takes shape,
With bugs and bees in funny shape!

The flowers chatter, oh what a scene,
As petals flap, they're quite the keen!
In every corner, life replays,
With nature's antics in the sun's warm rays.

Colors of a Leafy Revival

The trees don gowns of vibrant green,
In every shade, a festive scene.
They sway and wave, avoid the bees,
Who buzz around like wild cuties!

The dandelions prance with pride,
As grasshoppers jump and glide.
The petals giggle, the buds all cheer,
Is it spring, or a party here?

The tulips dance, the roses spin,
A botanical bash begins to win.
But watch your step and keep it light,
As worms hold dance-offs out of sight!

A squirrel's jive causes quite the fright,
As wildlife twirls in sheer delight.
In this blossom-bonanza play,
Laughs echo in the bright bouquet.

Beneath the Canopy of Renewal

Under the leaves where shadows mix,
The ants are having some strange tricks.
They form a train, they march about,
A leafy parade without a doubt!

The mushrooms giggle, wearing caps,
As raccoons' eyes sparkle, full of naps.
The earthworms flex their squiggly flair,
Beneath the soil, they play with care.

Sunshine filters through the trees,
While butterflies dance with the breeze.
Frogs leap out in flashy style,
As crickets chirp, they beguile!

Rustling leaves tell jokes anew,
As nature sings teamwork true.
What fun it is, this forest play,
Where lively critters guide the way!

Heartbeats of the Forest Floor

In the earthy depths, life thumps along,
With twigs that crack and critters that throng.
Mice scuttle fast, on a snack hunt spree,
While snails pass with wild glee!

The flowers yawn beneath the sun,
Who knew they could giggle, oh what fun!
Beneath the ferns, a dance floor glows,
With lichens and fungi in colors that pose.

The beetles boast in shiny attire,
While worms exchange tales getting higher.
The forest floor's a boisterous show,
With nature's rhythm and silly flow!

Each rustle and chirp, a light-hearted cheer,
As life rejoices, nothing to fear.
In this bustling buzz, the heart beats pure,
Where laughter blooms, of that we're sure!

Canvas of the Changing Seasons

Buds burst with laughter, what a sight!
Trees don their coats, green and bright.
Squirrels debate on how to dress,
As nature laughs, we must confess.

Pollen dances like it's in a ball,
Bees wear tiny hats, feeling quite tall.
Sunshine chuckles, warming our toes,
Underneath hats, the bloom gently grows.

Leaves yell "Frolic!" in vibrant glee,
While branches sway, like they're at a spree.
Every twig is a jester today,
In this woodland play, let's join the fray!

Nature's canvas, vivid and grand,
Splashing joy with a giggling hand.
What a riot, this seasonal art,
Let's paint the world, let's play our part!

Flickers of New Hope

A sprout peeks out, a curious chin,
"Hello, world!" with a cheeky grin.
Raindrops gossip as they splatter,
While worms wiggle, all in a chatter.

The sun starts to poke with a wink,
Clouds part ways to let him think.
Flowers giggle, shouting "Hooray!"
As bees buzz in, ready to play.

Little critters hold a parade,
Oh, the colors they've displayed!
Nature's joke is hard to miss;
"Why don't we dance?" asks a plump abyss.

With every seed, hope takes flight,
New beginnings springing bright.
So let's rejoice, it's time to cope,
In this carnival of flickers and hope!

The Regrowth Rhapsody

Once upon a trunk, a tale untold,
A tree stretches, breaking the mold.
Branches snap-joke, "We'll never fall!"
While roots chuckle, holding it all.

A new leaf whispers secrets and dreams,
Swaying along with the sun's bright beams.
Dandelions tease with their fluffy heads,
Grinning like jesters, making new beds.

Wiggly worms put on a show,
In the rich soil, they wiggle and flow.
"Who will win, the flower or me?"
They both laugh, "Let's wait and see!"

The forest hums a raucous tune,
In this saga beneath the moon.
With every sprout, a song's unfurled,
Welcome back to this whimsical world!

Fluttering Foliage

Leaves flutter down like confetti sprites,
Twirling and dancing in cheerful flights.
They high-five the wind, with playful bliss,
Each fall a celebration, none to miss.

Acorns roll by, wearing little caps,
While birdies chirp, taking friendly naps.
Nature's chuckle, a joyous sound,
As breezes dance through the playfully crowned.

Butterflies prance on a petal throne,
"Is this my cue?" a ladybug moans.
They flutter together, a giggling spree,
With laughter ringing through every tree.

So let's join hands with the leaves on the ground,
In this cheeky frolic, let's all come around.
With foliage flickering in vibrant displays,
Let the laughter of nature fill our days!

A Tapestry of Growth

In a garden of giggles, where daisies dance,
The trees tell jokes, give the squirrels a chance.
With whispers of leaves that tickle the breeze,
Nature wears laughter like a bright, leafy tease.

The sun plays peek-a-boo, hiding behind,
As roots play tag, oh what a find!
Branches swing low with a playful swoop,
While mushrooms giggle in their mushroomy group.

A bunny hops by in quirky parade,
Joining the fun that the flowers have made.
With colors that splash like a painter's delight,
Every bloom chuckles, catching the light.

The brook babbles tales of humor galore,
As frogs croak wisecracks from the muddy floor.
In this vibrant patch of the world gone wild,
Every life form is nature's own whimsical child.

The Language of the Verdant

The trees gossip softly in whispers and sighs,
While vines twist around with mischievous eyes.
Poppies wear hats made of soft, velvet dew,
As daisies toss petals, 'Hey! Look at you!'

The flowers converse in colors so bright,
Frogs on a lily pad have their own tune to write.
With bees buzzing talks, all in rhythmic hum,
Even the weeds can't help but join in the fun.

A squirrel mocks the grumpy old oak,
While tulips giggle at the old willow's smoke.
Breezes are laughter that carries the day,
And clouds grin down like kids at a play.

Every rustle and hum makes a vibrant song,
In this theater of green where all things belong.
Each leaf has a quirk, each root has a tale,
In this comedic garden, life will prevail.

Ripples of Awakening

As spring tiptoes in with a springy ballet,
The pond is alive, doing hip-hop today.
Frogs strike a pose on their lily pad thrones,
While goldfish chuckle in gurgling tones.

Buds pop open with a comedic flair,
Petals fall off as they dance in the air.
Each drop from the sky brings a splashy surprise,
While the worms in the earth giggle, oh my!

Grass tickles toes, a soft carpet of cheer,
A hedgehog rolls by, his laughter sincere.
Breezes chase dandelions, spun in delight,
This show of awakening ignites the night.

Nature's a jester, with jokes all around,
In the rippling stillness, joy can be found.
With each little bloom, a chorus of glee,
Embracing the humor in all that we see.

Secrets of the Old Growth

In the heart of the forest, secrets unfold,
With tall trees standing like stories retold.
The pine whispers riddles to acorns so spry,
As chips off the old block just wave and comply.

Moss covers ground like a fluffy green carpet,
Where chipmunks hold court and never seem outsmarted.
With branches like arms that reach for the sun,
The tales of the old woods are funny, not done.

The shadows giggle as they dance on the floor,
While owls wear glasses and act quite the bore.
Old growth is wise, but it knows how to jest,
With laughter that echoes, it's truly the best.

Each leaf knows a punchline, each twig has a laugh,
The woodland's a stage, where trees take a gaffe.
With whispers and chuckles, the forest's alive,
In the secret of growth, all creatures can thrive.

Reveries in Dappled Light

In dappled beams, the squirrels bounce,
Chasing sunbeams, they make their pounce.
Acorns fly like tiny grenades,
Nature's laughter, this parade.

The bees hum tunes of a buzzing choir,
While ants form lines, with their own desire.
A chipmunk slips on a sunny throne,
Declaring, 'This is my home alone!'

Leaves whisper jokes in a breezy jest,
Their rustling giggles never rest.
A robin sings, pretending to croon,
Its off-key notes make flowers swoon.

As sunlight dances through every bough,
Each critter's antics makes us say 'Wow!'
With every twist and every turn,
Nature's humor, how we yearn!

Embrace of the Opening Bloom

The flowers yawn, stretching wide and bright,
Telling tired buds, 'Get up, take flight!'
Daisies twirl like they're at a ball,
While tulips blush, standing proud and tall.

Catkins sway, with their fuzzy pride,
Whispering secrets to the breeze outside.
A bumblebee slips, landing so wrong,
It chuckles, 'Oops! I'll just hum along!'

Petals ruffle in a playful fight,
As colors clash, a comical sight.
In this garden, with laughter around,
Joyful blooms share laughs profound.

The sun grins down, its warmth a gift,
As butterflies gather for a good lift.
In the splash of hues, we see the play,
A festival of blooms come out to sway!

Scent of Fresh Earth

The earth inhales, rich and deep, and sways,
While worms work hard, planning their plays.
With scents so earthy, a cooking show,
'What's cooked today?' the daisies stow.

Mice peek out from their secret nooks,
Crafting mischief as they read their books.
They giggle to plants in a tuneful state,
Whispering secrets, 'Let's celebrate!'

As rain falls down in a slippery spree,
A puddle's formed, so wild and free.
Frogs leap in with exuberance bold,
Singing, 'Come join! It's a party, we're told!'

The sun breaks through, causing a stir,
To whiff those scents, oh what a blur!
In the dance of dirt, with life so spry,
Earth tells the story of joy and its high!

Tapestry of New Beginnings

From tiny seeds, the sprouts now peep,
Eagerly waiting, their secrets to keep.
Roots tickle the ground, saying 'Hello!'
While petals tease, 'Ready, set, go!'

A garden gnome takes a selfie in place,
With a grin so wide, oh, what a face!
Rabbits giggle, saying 'Cheese!'
Dancing around with the greatest of ease.

The ferns fidget, swaying left and right,
In a leafy conga, what a sight!
Their laughter echoing through the soft dew,
'Learning the groove, can you join too?'

As colors burst in a crazy swirl,
Nature's delight, a colorful whirl.
In every sprout, a joke to fling,
Celebrating life and the joy it will bring!

Buds of Brilliance

Tiny buds are popping out,
Like green balloons in a shout.
They wiggle, giggle, stretch so wide,
Inviting bees to join the ride.

Oh look, there's one that sneezed with flair,
A pollen puff, light as air.
It tickles my nose, I snort and sneeze,
The flowers laugh, they're taken with ease.

Buds with antics, all around,
In this garden, joy is found.
Petals wearing silly hats,
Flitting like chatty acrobats.

Nature's show, hilarious sight,
In this play, everything feels right.
Buds of brilliance, take a bow,
Your comedy, we cheer out loud!

Dance of the Dappled Sun

The sunlight dances on the beams,
Twisting shadows with bright gleams.
A squirrel spins a wiggly jig,
While worms do the worm, not so sprig!

Under leaves, laughter does abound,
With giggles hiding all around.
A bumblebee in sunglasses flies,
With a flower crown, oh what a surprise!

The sun takes breaks, like naps it seems,
The flowers gossip, sharing dreams.
Now a lizard joins the fun,
With dance moves that have just begun!

Nature's disco, wild and free,
A harmony of silly glee.
The dappled sun shines bright today,
As each creature comes out to play.

Unfurling Dreams

Out of dormancy, roots do yawn,
Tiny leaves push up at dawn.
With every wiggle, they declare,
"Let's hop and skip; we're almost there!"

A fern throws back its leafy hair,
Swaying side to side without a care.
While dandelions bloom in style,
Waving like they just ran a mile!

Midst the chaos, a beetle twirls,
On daisies with their little curls.
While butterflies, like dancers bright,
Floated past with pure delight.

So here's to dreams that dare to climb,
In the wild, we know it's time.
Unfurl your hopes, don't hesitate,
Let nature giggle, it's not too late!

The Tender Green Uprising

A riot of green, in every nook,
A leafy insurrection, take a look!
The sprouts unite, forming a crew,
With potted plants joining, too!

Lettuce leads with a green beret,
Cauliflower joins, come what may!
Tomatoes cheer, with smiles so bright,
As flowers prepare for their big fight!

The roots are ready to dig in deep,
While garden gnomes giggle, not asleep.
A carrot sings, "Let's raise some cheer!"
The world's our stage, no need for fear!

In this uprising, joy must reign,
As nature throws down a funny chain.
The tender greens proclaim their score,
"Together, we will flourish more!"

Awakening Earth

Beneath the soil, a tickle grows,
Earthworms giggle as the sun glows.
Tiny buds are making their plans,
Even squirrels are lending their hands.

The daisies dance with a silly sway,
Tugging at grass like it's play day.
Blades of green are pulling tight,
Rooted in laughter, they stretch with delight.

A dandelion hops in the breeze,
Planting its seeds just like it's a tease.
The bees wear hats, buzzing with glee,
"Hey, who's throwing pollen at me?"

So here we are, laughing in bloom,
Nature's comedy breaks any gloom.
With every sprout waving goodbye,
Spring's a punchline that makes us fly!

The Promise of Petals

Blossoms peek through a curtain of green,
Giggling flowers planning a scene.
Petals like socks tossed in the air,
Tulips tease the breeze without a care.

A rose grins wide, then turns to a bud,
"I've got thorns but I still feel good!"
The daisies chant in ridiculous rhyme,
"We'll bloom so bright, just give us time!"

A sunflower jokes, tall as a house,
"I'll wave at the birds, being their spouse!"
Nature's humor spills out like juice,
With every color, there's no excuse.

Petals in blues, yellows, and red,
Might just slip into laughter instead.
Spring's bouquet's a jester's delight,
Promising fun until dusk meets night!

Awakening the Heartwood

Deep in the woods, trees whisper and giggle,
"Watch out, it's spring!" they all start to wiggle.
Bark-covered jokers sharing their tales,
Roots tickling each other, sending out trails.

Leaves popping out, dressed in bright suits,
"Did we miss the party? Let's raise our roots!"
Branches stretch wide, and the squirrels all cheer,
"Climb up, get down, let's drink some root beer!"

Birds clock in for their morning flight,
Tweeting and chirping, what a grand sight.
"Who needs a lodge when you've a free tree?
Join us up here, and let's all just be!"

With heartwood alive, the laughter won't cease,
Nature's connection is purest with ease.
So let's leap and dance, let's shout and proclaim,
In this lively forest, we're all part of the game!

Symphony of Sprouts

In the garden, a melody hums,
As seeds start to giggle and plump into chums.
Carrots are tap dancing deep in the ground,
While radishes blush, hiding around.

Sunshine drops notes as flowers all sway,
Each petal a drummer in bright disarray.
Beets keep the rhythm with wobbly beats,
Making sure everyone's tapping their feet.

The peas in the pods crack up and conspire,
"Who knew being green could take us so higher?"
A radish proclaims in its snazzy red coat,
"Join us for fun on this veggie-like boat!"

In this vibrant show, we embrace every sound,
Where laughter and growth can both be found.
Let's bloom and let's blossom with everyone's heart,
In this symphony of sprouts, we all play a part!

A Symphony of Renewal

In spring, the trees giggle and sway,
Their branches dance in a crazy ballet.
Squirrels boast of their nutty treasure,
While birds chirp in wild, silly pleasure.

The blossoms burst in a colorful spree,
Bees buzz around like they're wild with glee.
Leaves rustle with secrets, oh what a tease,
Nature's own jesters, putting us at ease.

The flowers compete for the sun's warm grin,
Petals flutter like they're wearing a pin.
Watch out for the bloom that sneezes too loud,
Making the nearby boughs wiggle and bow!

So dance, dear trees, in your leafy attire,
Join in the jest like you're a live wire.
Springtime's festival of laughter anew,
Here's to the green comedies meant just for you!

Secrets from the Boughs Below

Under the leaves, the critters conspire,
Plotting mischief that could raise a quire.
A rabbit bursts out with a chuckle so bright,
As the hedgehog plans a wild midnight flight.

Caterpillars gossip of their coming flight,
While the ants march like they own the night.
A snickering squirrel hides acorns with flair,
Claiming 'It's mine!' with a devil-may-care.

The tree trunks lean in, sharing a laugh,
As saplings plot for a new photograph.
"Say cheese!" through the giggles, a soft creak is heard,
As roots rumble low, like a tickled bird.

With whispers that tickle the cold, damp air,
Every twig has a tale, fable to share.
So lean in close, hear the chuckles they weave,
For nature's a joker on this spring eve!

Whispers of the Awakening Grove

In the grove where the sun spills a golden glow,
The flowers gossip, their colors in tow.
"Hey there, tall oak, lost a branch in the breeze?"
"I prefer to call it a hairstyle that frees!"

Breezes nudge leaves with sweet little pokes,
Tickling the bobbing, frolicking folks.
The mushrooms chuckle as they grow in a line,
Winking at ladybugs sipping on wine.

Beetles strut like they're in a parade,
Waving their tiny arms, proud and displayed.
A forgot-me-not laughs, "I've bloomed out of turn!"
"I'm just fashionably late," the petals discern.

The grove chuckles, echoing laughter so bright,
Every rustle and giggle gives springtime delight.
So gather your joy, let the mirth intertwine,
For nature's a party, let's all sip and dine!

Roots of Renewal

Deep in the soil where the secrets reside,
The roots have begun a jubilant ride.
"Let's throw a bash, invite all earth's critters!"
As moles tap their toes, adding to the litters.

A worm wobbles, doing its best twist,
While beetles form pairs, joining in the list.
"Come one, come all, to the party down low!"
"Bring your best dance moves, put on your best show!"

With laughter that bubbles from ancient old trees,
And whispers from moss as soft as a breeze.
Roots wiggle and jiggle, a tactile affair,
In the underground ball, there's life everywhere!

So cheer for the roots, in their earthy domain,
As they revel below, through sunshine and rain.
For spring brings new life, and giggles galore,
In this whimsical space, there's always much more!

www.ingramcontent.com/pod-product-compliance
Lightning Source LLC
Chambersburg PA
CBHW071813160426
43209CB00003B/65